Tender Hearts: Navigating the Journey of Caring for an Elderly Parent or Grandparent

Jill Wyatt

ISBN: 9798389905238

DEDICATION

To my beloved grandmother, Gertrude DuBois,

At 96 years old, you may be losing your sight and hearing, but your moments of clarity, strength, and wisdom continue to inspire me every day. This book is dedicated to you and the countless other elderly parents and grandparents who deserve the love and care you have given us throughout your life. May this book serve as a tribute to your resilience and an inspiration to all those who care for their elderly loved ones.

CONTENTS

ACKNOWLEDGMENTS

I would like to express my heartfelt gratitude to the following people who have supported me in writing this book:

To my beloved grandmother, Gertrude DuBois, thank you for being the inspiration behind this book. Your strength and resilience in the face of adversity inspire me daily.

To my mother, Wanda Grote, thank you for your unwavering support and encouragement throughout nursing school and the writing of this book. Your own experiences in caring for our family have inspired me to help others through this journey.

To my husband, Richard Wyatt Jr., thank you for supporting me in everything I dream of doing, including pursuing my career in nursing and writing this book. Your love and encouragement mean the world to me.

I would also like to extend my appreciation to my colleagues and fellow caregivers who have shared their insights and experiences with me throughout the years. Without your guidance and support, this book would not have been possible.

Lastly, I want to thank the readers who have chosen to read this book. It is my hope that the information and guidance provided within these pages will help you navigate the journey of caring for your elderly loved one with greater confidence, understanding, and compassion.

INTRODUCTION

Tender Hearts: Navigating the Journey of Caring for an Elderly Parent or Grandparent was born out of a desire to provide support and guidance to those who are caring for their elderly loved ones. As a certified nurse assistant with experience in long-term care and mental health care, I have seen firsthand the challenges that come with being a caregiver, and I understand how overwhelming it can be to navigate the physical, emotional, financial, and legal aspects of caring for an elderly parent or grandparent.

This book is the result of my personal experience as a caregiver, as well as my professional expertise in the healthcare industry. I was inspired to write this book after witnessing the struggles my mother faced when we decided to move my grandmother into our home. Although I was familiar with the aging process and the challenges that come with being a caregiver, my mother was not fully prepared for the physical and emotional toll that caring for an elderly loved one can take.

Tender Hearts is a comprehensive guide that delves into the everyday trials and tribulations that caregivers face when taking care of their elderly loved ones. It provides practical advice and insights into the physical, emotional, cognitive, financial, and legal aspects of caregiving, as well as the importance of self-care for caregivers themselves. By sharing my personal and professional experiences, I hope to offer a sense of comfort, support, and understanding to those who are on this journey with their loved ones.

I hope this book will serve as a valuable resource for anyone caring for an elderly parent or grandparent. It is my sincere hope that the information contained within these pages will help to alleviate some of the stress and uncertainty that comes with caregiving and empower you to provide the best care possible for your loved one while also taking care of yourself.

Tender Hearts: Navigating the Journey of Caring for an Elderly Parent is a comprehensive guide that aims to provide support, advice, and insights into caregiving's emotional, physical, cognitive, financial, and legal aspects and the importance of self-care for caregivers. As you embark on this new journey, this book will help you understand the range of emotions that may arise and offer guidance on navigating these feelings while maintaining a healthy mindset. Becoming a caregiver for an elderly parent is a life-altering experience filled with a range of emotions, challenges, and rewards. As you embark on this journey, it is crucial to understand the complexities of caregiving, accept your new role, and develop a healthy mindset that will enable you to provide the best care possible for your loved one. This book will guide you through understanding caregiving, coping with the common emotions experienced by caregivers, and establishing a positive approach to care.

Understanding the Caregiving Journey

The caregiving journey is unique for every individual, shaped by factors such as the specific needs of your elderly parent, the support system you have in place, and your own personal experiences. Therefore, as you begin this journey, it is essential to:

- Learn about your parent's needs: Educate yourself about your parent's medical conditions, physical limitations, and cognitive challenges to better understand their care requirements.

- Assess your capabilities: Honestly evaluate your strengths, limitations, and resources to determine what kind of care you can provide and where you may need additional support.

- Build a support system: Establish a network of friends, family, and professionals who can offer assistance, advice, and encouragement throughout your caregiving journey.

Coping with Common Emotions Experienced by Caregivers

As a caregiver, you will likely encounter a wide range of emotions, such as:

- Love and compassion: Strong feelings of love and compassion may motivate you to provide the best care possible for your parent.

- Guilt and frustration: You may experience guilt or frustration when faced with the limitations of your caregiving abilities or when your parent's condition worsens.

- Grief and loss: Caregiving often involves grieving the loss of your parent's independence, cognitive abilities, or the relationship you once had.

- Worry and stress: Concerns about your parent's well-being and the future and balancing your own life can lead to worry and stress.

Developing a Healthy Mindset for Caregiving

To cultivate a healthy mindset for caregiving, consider the following strategies:

- Set realistic expectations: Recognize that caregiving has limitations, and accept that some aspects of your parent's care may be beyond your control.

- Practice self-compassion: Treat yourself with kindness and understanding, acknowledging that caregiving is challenging and you are doing your best.
- Stay flexible and adaptable: Be prepared to adjust your caregiving approach as your parent's needs change, and remain open to learning and growth.
- Prioritize self-care: Ensure you care for your physical, emotional, and mental well-being to maintain your resilience and ability to care for your parent.

As you embark on your caregiving journey, embracing your new role, coping with the emotions that arise, and cultivating a healthy mindset are essential steps toward providing the best possible care for your elderly parent. This introductory chapter serves as a foundation for the rest of the book, which delves deeper into the many aspects of caregiving, offering practical advice, support, and insights to help you navigate this significant life change. Remember, you are not alone on this journey, and support is available to help you every step of the way.

2 EMBRACING YOUR NEW ROLE AS A CAREGIVER

As you transition into the role of caregiver and understand the importance of accepting this new responsibility. It covers common feelings and emotions experienced by caregivers, such as guilt, frustration, and worry, and provides guidance on coping with these emotions healthily. The caregiving journey is an emotional and transformative experience filled with love, compassion, and determination. As you step into the role of caregiver for your elderly parent, it is essential to embrace this new responsibility and understand the emotional landscape that comes with it. We will explore the familiar feelings and emotions experienced by caregivers, discuss the significance of accepting your new role, and provide guidance on coping with these emotions healthily and constructively.

The Emotional Landscape of Caregiving

As a caregiver, you are likely to encounter a wide range of emotions shaped by your unique experiences and the specific challenges faced by your elderly parent. Some of the most common emotions experienced by caregivers include:

- Love and compassion: Your deep love for your parent and compassion toward their struggles can fuel your motivation to provide the best care.
- Guilt: Many caregivers feel guilt for not doing enough, feeling overwhelmed by their responsibilities, or any negative emotions that may arise during caregiving.
- Frustration: Caregiving can be frustrating, especially when dealing with challenging behaviors, lack of progress, or unmet expectations.
- Worry: It's natural to worry about your parent's well-being, their future, and the impact of caregiving on your own life and relationships.
- Grief and loss: Caregivers often experience grief over losing their parent's independence, cognitive abilities, or the relationship they once had.
- Exhaustion: Physical and emotional fatigue can take a toll on caregivers, making it challenging to maintain a positive outlook and continue providing care.

Accepting Your New Role as a Caregiver

Embracing your new role as a caregiver involves acknowledging the change in your relationship with your elderly parent and accepting the responsibilities that come with caregiving. To accept your new role, consider the following strategies:

- Acknowledge the change: Recognize that becoming a caregiver is a significant shift in your relationship with your parent and will require adjustments in your daily life and responsibilities.
- Educate yourself: Learn about your parent's specific needs, conditions, and the caregiving tasks you will be responsible for to better prepare yourself for the journey ahead.

- Develop a caregiving plan: Create a plan outlining your parent's care needs, responsibilities, and the support system you will rely on. This will help you feel more organized and in control.

- Be patient with yourself: Understand that adjusting to your new role will take time, and allow yourself the grace to learn and adapt as you go.

Coping with Emotions in a Healthy Way

As you navigate the emotional landscape of caregiving, managing your emotions in a healthy and constructive manner is essential. To cope with your emotions, consider the following tips:

- Accept your feelings: Acknowledge and validate your emotions, understanding that they are a natural part of the caregiving process. Allow yourself to experience these feelings without judgment or guilt.

- Seek support: Share your feelings with friends, family members, or support groups who can offer understanding, advice, and encouragement. Talking about your emotions can help you process them and gain new perspectives.

- Practice self-compassion: Be kind to yourself, recognizing that caregiving is challenging and you are doing your best. Remind yourself that it's okay to feel overwhelmed or frustrated at times and that these feelings don't make you a bad caregiver.

- Engage in self-care: Prioritize your own well-being by engaging in activities that bring you joy and relaxation. This includes exercising, spending time with friends and loved ones, pursuing hobbies, or practicing mindfulness and relaxation techniques. Taking care of yourself helps you better manage your emotions and maintain the energy and resilience needed for caregiving.

- Set realistic expectations: Understand that there will be limitations to what you can do as a caregiver and that some aspects of your parent's care may be beyond your control. By setting realistic expectations, you can reduce feelings of guilt and frustration when things don't go as planned.

- Focus on the positive: Celebrate small victories and moments of joy in your caregiving journey. Acknowledging your achievements and positive impact on your parent's life can help counterbalance negative emotions.

- Seek professional help if needed: If your emotions become overwhelming or interfere with your daily life, consider seeking professional help from a therapist or counselor specializing in caregiver support.

The Importance of Emotional Resilience

Emotional resilience is the ability to adapt and cope with stress and adversity, which is crucial for caregivers as they navigate the challenges of their role. To build emotional resilience, consider the following strategies:

- Cultivate a strong support system: Surround yourself with people who understand your caregiving journey and can provide emotional support, encouragement, and practical assistance when needed.

- Practice stress-reducing techniques: Engage in activities that help reduce stress, such as mindfulness, deep breathing exercises, or progressive muscle relaxation.

- Maintain a sense of humor: Laughter can be a powerful coping mechanism, helping to diffuse tension and lighten the emotional load.

- Focus on what you can control: Recognize that some aspects of caregiving will be beyond your control, and focus your energy on the areas where you can make a positive difference.

- Embrace a growth mindset: View challenges as opportunities for personal growth and learning rather than insurmountable obstacles.

Embracing your new role as a caregiver is a journey filled with love, compassion, and determination. As you navigate the emotional landscape of caregiving, remember to accept your feelings, seek support, and practice self-care to maintain a healthy mindset. By cultivating emotional resilience and learning to cope with the challenges that come with caregiving, you will be better equipped to provide the best possible care for your elderly parent

3 UNDERSTANDING THE NEEDS OF YOUR ELDERLY PARENT

Caring for elderly parents requires a deep understanding of their unique physical, emotional, and cognitive needs. In addition, as your parent ages, they may face various age-related challenges, impacting their overall well-being and quality of life. In this chapter, we will explore the common age-related challenges seniors face, including mobility issues, chronic pain, memory loss, and social isolation, and provide practical advice for compassionately and effectively addressing these needs.

Physical Needs of Elderly Parents

As your parent ages, they may experience various physical changes and challenges that can impact their daily life and independence. Some of the most common physical needs of elderly parents include the following:

- Mobility and balance issues: Aging can lead to decreased muscle strength, flexibility, and balance, making it difficult for your parent to move around safely and comfortably. They may need assistance walking, transferring, or navigating their living environment.

- Chronic pain: Older adults often experience chronic pain due to conditions such as arthritis, osteoporosis, or nerve damage. This pain can impact their ability to perform daily activities and affect their overall quality of life.

- Sensory changes: Aging can result in changes to vision, hearing, and touch, making it challenging for your parent to process and interpret sensory information.

- Nutritional needs: Elderly parents may have unique nutritional needs, such as increased calcium intake for bone health or reduced sodium intake for blood pressure management. They may also experience changes in appetite, taste, or digestion that can impact their ability to consume a balanced diet.

- Medication management: Older adults often take multiple medications to manage chronic health conditions, making it essential to properly manage and monitor their medication regimen to avoid potential complications or adverse effects.

Emotional Needs of Elderly Parents

As your parent ages, they may also experience emotional challenges that can impact their mental health and well-being. Some of the most common emotional needs of elderly parents include the following:

- Social connection: Maintaining social relationships is crucial for your parent's emotional well-being. As they age, they may experience increased social isolation due to losing friends, limited mobility, or the inability to participate in activities they once enjoyed.

- A sense of purpose: Many older adults struggle with finding a purpose as they retire from work, experience the "empty nest" syndrome, or lose their independence. This can lead to feelings of loneliness, depression, or low self-worth.

- Grief and loss: Aging often involves experiencing various forms of loss, such as the death of loved ones, the decline in physical abilities, or the loss of independence. These losses can lead to feelings of grief, sadness, and despair.

- Adjustment to change: Your parent may struggle

with adapting to the changes that come with aging, such as moving to a new living environment, relying on others for assistance, or accepting their physical limitations.

Cognitive Needs of Elderly Parents

Cognitive changes are expected as your parent ages, and they can impact their ability to think, reason, and remember information. Some of the most common cognitive needs of elderly parents include the following:

- Memory loss: Age-related memory loss can range from mild forgetfulness to more severe cognitive decline, such as dementia or Alzheimer's disease. This can impact your parent's ability to recall information, manage daily tasks, or engage in meaningful conversations.

- Decision-making: Older adults may experience difficulties with decision-making, problem-solving, or planning, which can impact their ability to manage their finances, make healthcare decisions, or navigate their daily life.

- Attention and concentration: Aging can result in decreased attention span and difficulty concentrating, making it challenging for your parent to focus on tasks, engage in conversations, or process new information. This can affect their ability to stay organized, follow instructions, or participate in activities they previously enjoyed.

Strategies for Addressing the Needs of Your Elderly Parent

Now that we have explored the common physical, emotional, and cognitive needs of elderly parents, let's discuss some practical strategies for addressing these needs in a compassionate and effective manner:

- Encourage physical activity: Engaging in regular physical activity can help your parent maintain muscle strength, flexibility, and balance, reducing their risk of falls and improving their overall well-being. Work with your parent's healthcare provider to develop a safe and appropriate exercise routine tailored to their abilities and interests.

- Manage chronic pain: Collaborate with your parent's healthcare team to develop a comprehensive pain management plan, which may include a combination of medication, physical therapy, and alternative therapies such as massage or acupuncture.

- Address sensory changes: Ensure your parent's living environment accommodates their sensory needs by providing adequate lighting, clear signage, and non-slip surfaces. Encourage regular eye and hearing exams, and consider assistive devices such as hearing aids or magnifying glasses if needed.

- Provide nutritious meals: Work with a dietitian or nutritionist to create a balanced meal plan that meets your parent's unique nutritional needs. Encourage regular, small meals and provide a variety of flavors and textures to stimulate their appetite.

- Assist with medication management: Help your parent create and maintain an up-to-date medication list, including dosages and administration instructions. Consider using a pill organizer or setting reminders to ensure they take their medications as prescribed.

- Facilitate social connections: Encourage your parent to engage in social activities, such as attending senior center events, joining clubs or support groups, or connecting with friends and family. If needed, offer transportation or assistance with technology to help them stay connected.

- Encourage a sense of purpose: Help your parent

identify activities, hobbies, or volunteer opportunities that align with their interests and abilities, providing them with a sense of purpose and accomplishment.

- Offer emotional support: Be an empathetic listener and validate your parent's feelings as they navigate the challenges of aging. If needed, encourage them to share their emotions and seek professional help, such as therapy or counseling.

- Provide cognitive stimulation: Engage your parent in activities that promote cognitive health, such as puzzles, games, reading, or learning new skills. Encourage social interaction and participation in mentally stimulating activities to help keep their mind sharp.

- Be patient and flexible: Understand that your parent's needs may change over time, and be willing to adapt your approach as needed. Communicate openly and honestly with your parent and healthcare team to ensure the best care.

Understanding and addressing the physical, emotional, and cognitive needs of your elderly parent is crucial to providing them with the best possible care and support. You can help your parent maintain their health, well-being, and independence throughout their golden years by being attentive to their unique challenges and working collaboratively with healthcare professionals.

4 PHYSICAL CARE: HELPING THEM STAY HEALTHY AND COMFORTABLE

Caring for the physical well-being of your elderly parent is a crucial aspect of your role as a caregiver. Ensuring they are healthy, comfortable, and safe requires attention to their personal hygiene, medication management, and nutritional needs. In this chapter, we will explore the everyday tasks involved in providing physical care for your elderly parent and offer practical advice for performing these tasks effectively and compassionately.

Personal Hygiene and Grooming

Maintaining good personal hygiene and grooming is essential for your parent's health, comfort, and self-esteem. In addition, as a caregiver, you may need to assist your parent with various personal care tasks, such as:

- Bathing and showering: Many elderly individuals have difficulty bathing or showering independently due to mobility issues, balance problems, or fear of slipping. Assist your parent with bathing or showering as needed, ensuring their safety and preserving their dignity. Consider using a shower chair, grab bars, or non-slip mats to create a safer environment.

- Oral care: Proper oral hygiene is essential for maintaining overall health and preventing infections. Help your parent with brushing their teeth, flossing, and using mouthwash, if necessary. Ensure they have regular dental checkups and address any dental concerns promptly.

- Hair care: Assist your parent with washing, combing, or styling their hair, as needed. Regular haircuts and grooming can help boost their self-esteem and overall well-being.

- Nail care: Trim your parent's fingernails and toenails regularly to prevent ingrown nails and infections. If they have diabetes or other health conditions that affect their circulation, seek guidance from their healthcare provider before trimming their nails.

- Skincare: Keep your parent's skin clean and moisturized to prevent dryness, irritation, or pressure sores. Regularly inspect their skin for signs of redness, swelling, or infection, and address any concerns with their healthcare provider.

- Toileting and continence care: Assist your parent with using the toilet or managing incontinence, if necessary. Be patient and understanding, offering reassurance and privacy to preserve their dignity. Discuss any continence issues with their healthcare provider and explore options for managing incontinence, such as disposable briefs, pads, or scheduled toileting.

Medication Management

Proper medication management is vital to your parent's health and safety. As a caregiver, you may need to help your parent manage their medications, which may involve:

- Organizing medications: Create and maintain an up-to-date list of your parent's medications, including dosages, administration instructions, and any potential side effects or interactions. Consider using a pill organizer to sort their medications by day and time.

- Administering medications: Ensure your parent takes their medications as prescribed, providing assistance with swallowing or opening medication containers, if necessary. Set reminders or alarms to help them stay on schedule.

- Monitoring for side effects: Keep an eye out for any potential side effects or adverse reactions to your parent's medications. Report any concerns to their healthcare provider promptly.

- Managing prescription refills: Keep track of your parent's medication supply and ensure they have enough medication to last until their next refill. Coordinate with their healthcare provider and pharmacy to obtain refills as needed.

- Staying informed: Educate yourself about your parent's medications and stay informed about any changes to their medication regimen. Communicate with their healthcare team and ask questions about a medication's purpose, dosage, or administration instructions.

Nutrition and Meal Preparation

Providing nutritious meals is essential for maintaining your parent's health and well-being. As a caregiver, you may need to plan, prepare, and serve meals that meet your elderly parent's unique nutritional needs. This can involve:

- Understanding their dietary requirements: Consult with a dietitian or nutritionist to determine the appropriate caloric intake, macronutrient balance, and any specific dietary restrictions or considerations for your parent. Consider factors such as age, weight, activity level, and medical conditions when planning their meals.

- Creating a meal plan: Develop a weekly meal plan that incorporates a variety of nutrient-dense foods, such as lean proteins, whole grains, fruits, vegetables, and healthy fats. Aim for balanced meals that are visually appealing and cater to your parent's taste preferences.

- Grocery shopping: Purchase high-quality, fresh ingredients to prepare meals for your parent. Consider their dietary needs and preferences when shopping for groceries, and choose foods that are easy to chew, swallow, and digest if they have difficulty with these tasks.

- Preparing meals: Cook meals that are both nutritious and enjoyable for your parent. Adapt recipes or cooking methods as needed to accommodate their dietary restrictions, taste preferences, or difficulty with chewing or swallowing.

- Encouraging hydration: Ensure your parent drinks adequate fluids throughout the day to maintain proper hydration. Offer a variety of beverages, such as water, milk, juice, or tea, and consider using a straw or sippy cup if they have difficulty drinking from a regular cup.

- Assisting with eating: If your parent has difficulty feeding themselves, provide assistance with cutting food, using utensils, or bringing food to their mouth. Be patient and encouraging, offering gentle prompts and reassurance as needed.

- Monitoring their nutritional status: Regularly assess your parent's weight, appetite, and overall health to ensure they are receiving adequate nutrition. Discuss any concerns or changes in their nutritional status with their healthcare provider.

Sleep and Rest

Adequate sleep and rest are essential for maintaining your elderly parent's physical health and emotional well-being. As a caregiver, you may need to:

- Create a comfortable sleep environment: Ensure your parent's bedroom is quiet, dark, and a comfortable temperature for sleeping. Provide a supportive mattress and pillows, and consider using adaptive equipment, such as bed rails or a bedside commode, if needed.

- Establish a bedtime routine: Encourage your parent to develop a consistent bedtime routine that includes winding down activities, such as reading, listening to calming music, or taking a warm bath.

- Address sleep disturbances: If your parent experiences difficulty falling asleep or staying asleep, discuss these issues with their healthcare provider. Consider potential causes, such as pain, medication side effects, or sleep disorders, and explore appropriate interventions to improve their sleep quality.

- Encourage regular rest periods: Encourage your parent to take regular breaks and rest periods throughout the day to conserve energy and prevent fatigue.

Providing physical care for your elderly parent is a critical aspect of your role as a caregiver. By assisting with personal hygiene, managing medications, preparing nutritious meals, and promoting adequate sleep and rest, you can help your parent maintain their health, comfort, and overall well-being. Remember to be patient, compassionate, and adaptive in your approach, and work closely with your parent's healthcare team to ensure they receive the best possible care

5 EMOTIONAL CARE: NURTURING THEIR HEART AND SOUL

Providing emotional care for your elderly parent is a critical aspect of your role as a caregiver. Emotional support and companionship are essential for maintaining their mental and emotional well-being, contributing to their overall quality of life. In this chapter, we will discuss the importance of empathy, patience, and communication in building a solid emotional bond with your elderly parent and offer guidance on how to provide emotional care that nurtures their heart and soul.

Building Empathy and Understanding

Empathy is the ability to understand and share the feelings of another person. Developing empathy for your elderly parent's experiences and emotions is crucial for providing compassionate emotional care. To build empathy and understanding, consider the following strategies:

- Listen actively: When your parent talks about their feelings, thoughts, or concerns, give them your full attention. Listen without interrupting or offering unsolicited advice, and validate their emotions by acknowledging their feelings and expressing understanding.

- Put yourself in their shoes: Try to imagine what it might be like to experience your parent's physical, emotional, and cognitive challenges. This can help you better understand their emotions and needs and respond with compassion and sensitivity.

- Educate yourself: Learn about the aging process, common age-related challenges, and the emotional impact of these challenges on seniors. This knowledge can help you develop empathy for your parent's experiences and inform your approach to providing emotional care.

Cultivating Patience and Compassion

As a caregiver, it is crucial to practice patience and compassion when providing emotional care for your elderly parent. Patience allows you to maintain a calm and supportive demeanor, even in challenging situations, while compassion enables you to respond with kindness and understanding. To cultivate patience and compassion, consider the following strategies:

- Take a deep breath: When you feel frustrated or impatient, pause and take a few deep breaths to help you regain your composure and refocus on providing compassionate care.

- Set realistic expectations: Understand that your parent may have limitations due to their age, health, or cognitive function. Adjust your expectations accordingly and recognize that they may need more time, assistance, or support to complete tasks or express their feelings.

- Practice self-compassion: Remember that caregiving can be challenging, and sometimes it is natural to feel overwhelmed or frustrated. Acknowledge your feelings without judgment and treat yourself with kindness and understanding.

Effective Communication

Effective communication is essential for building a strong emotional bond with your elderly parent and providing emotional care that meets their needs. To enhance your communication skills, consider the following strategies:

- Use open-ended questions: Encourage your parent to share their thoughts and feelings by asking open-ended questions that require more than a yes or no answer. For example, ask, "How are you feeling today?" or "What did you enjoy most about our visit to the park?"

- Be mindful of nonverbal cues: Pay attention to your parent's body language, facial expressions, and tone of voice, as these can provide valuable insights into their emotional state. Adjust your communication style and approach based on their nonverbal cues to better connect with them.

- Speak clearly and simply: Use clear, concise language and speak at a comfortable pace and volume for your parent. Break down complex information or instructions into smaller, more manageable steps, and use repetition and reinforcement as needed to ensure understanding.

- Validate their emotions: When your parent expresses their feelings, validate them by acknowledging them and expressing understanding. For example, say, "It sounds like you're feeling lonely today. I can understand why you might feel that way."

Providing Emotional Support and Companionship

As a caregiver, one of your primary responsibilities is to offer emotional support and companionship to your elderly parent. You can help your parent feel valued, connected, and cared for by being present, engaged, and understanding. To provide emotional support and companionship, consider the following strategies:

- Spend quality time together: Set aside time each

day to engage with your parent in meaningful activities, such as reading, playing games, or simply chatting. These shared experiences can strengthen your emotional bond and provide your parent with a sense of belonging and purpose.

- Encourage social interaction: Help your parent maintain their social connections by facilitating visits with friends and family members, organizing outings to community events, or encouraging participation in group activities. Social interaction can promote emotional well-being and help combat feelings of loneliness and isolation.

- Offer a listening ear: Be available when your parent wants to discuss their feelings, thoughts, or concerns. Offer comfort and reassurance, and avoid minimizing or dismissing their emotions.

- Provide emotional validation: Acknowledge and validate your parent's emotions, even if you do not necessarily agree with their perspective. This can help your parent feel heard and understood, fostering a sense of trust and connection between you.

- Be patient and flexible: As your parent's needs and emotions may fluctuate, it is essential to be patient and flexible in your approach to providing emotional care. Adapt your communication style, level of support, and caregiving strategies as needed to meet their changing needs.

- Seek professional help when necessary: If your parent is experiencing significant emotional distress, such as symptoms of depression or anxiety, consult with their healthcare provider or a mental health professional. Early intervention can help address emotional challenges and improve your parent's overall well-being.

Providing emotional care for your elderly parent is a

vital aspect of your role as a caregiver. By developing empathy and understanding, cultivating patience and compassion, enhancing your communication skills, and offering emotional support and companionship, you can nurture your parent's heart and soul and help them maintain a positive emotional state. Remember that emotional care is an ongoing process, and it is essential to continually assess your parent's emotional well-being and adjust your caregiving strategies as needed to ensure they receive the support they need.

6 COGNITIVE CARE: ENGAGING THEIR MIND

Maintaining cognitive health is essential for promoting the overall well-being of your elderly parent. As a caregiver, you play a vital role in providing cognitive stimulation and engaging their mind to help delay cognitive decline and enhance their mental function. This chapter will explore various activities and strategies to keep your parent's mind sharp and engaged, such as puzzles, games, and meaningful conversations.

Understanding Cognitive Health in Aging

As people age, they may experience a decline in cognitive function, which can manifest as memory loss, difficulty concentrating, or slower processing speed. However, research has shown that engaging in mentally stimulating activities can help maintain cognitive health and slow cognitive decline. As a caregiver, you can support your parent's cognitive health by providing various cognitive activities and promoting a mentally stimulating environment.

Cognitive Activities for Elderly Parents

There are numerous activities that can help keep your

parent's mind sharp and engaged. Some examples include:

- Puzzles: Jigsaw puzzles, crossword puzzles, and Sudoku puzzles are excellent options for promoting problem-solving skills and mental dexterity.

- Board games and card games: Games like Scrabble, chess, checkers, and bridge can help improve concentration, memory, and strategic thinking.

- Reading and writing: Encourage your parent to read books, newspapers, or magazines and engage in writing activities such as journaling, poetry, or letter writing.

- Arts and crafts: Activities like painting, drawing, knitting, or sewing can stimulate creativity and help maintain fine motor skills.

- Hobbies and interests: Help your parent explore new hobbies or continue existing interests, such as gardening, cooking, or playing a musical instrument.

Encouraging Meaningful Conversations

Meaningful conversations can help keep your elderly parent's mind active and engaged. To foster stimulating conversations:

- Ask open-ended questions: Encourage your parent to share their thoughts and opinions by asking open-ended questions that require more than a yes or no answer.

- Discuss current events: Engage your parent in discussions about news, politics, or community events to promote critical thinking and awareness.

- Share memories: Reminiscing about the past can help your parent exercise their memory and reinforce their sense of identity.

- Encourage storytelling: Invite your parent to share stories from their life, which can promote cognitive function and strengthen your emotional connection.

Adapting Activities for Cognitive Abilities

It is essential to tailor cognitive activities to your parent's abilities and preferences. Keep the following considerations in mind:

- Consider their cognitive level: Choose activities that are appropriate for your parent's cognitive abilities and modify tasks as needed to ensure they are engaging but not overly frustrating.

- Be mindful of sensory limitations: If your parent has vision or hearing impairments, select activities that accommodate their sensory limitations.

- Encourage a sense of accomplishment: Break tasks into smaller, manageable steps and provide guidance and support as needed to help your parent experience a sense of accomplishment and build confidence in their abilities.

- Monitor for signs of fatigue or frustration: Be attentive to your parent's emotional state and adjust activities or provide breaks as needed to prevent fatigue or frustration.

Creating a Mentally Stimulating Environment

In addition to providing specific cognitive activities, you can promote cognitive health by creating a mentally stimulating environment for your elderly parent. Some strategies include:

- Encourage social interaction: Social engagement is crucial for cognitive health. Facilitate opportunities for your parent to connect with friends, family, or community members.

- Provide access to mentally stimulating materials: Ensure your parent has access to a variety of cognitive resources, such as books, newspapers, puzzles, and educational or engaging multimedia content. This can include documentaries, podcasts, audiobooks, and online resources or apps designed to stimulate cognitive function.

Cognitive care is a vital aspect of caregiving for elderly parents. By understanding their cognitive needs and engaging their minds through various activities and conversations, you can help maintain and support their mental health. Keep in mind that each individual's cognitive abilities and preferences may vary, so it is crucial to tailor activities accordingly and create a mentally stimulating environment that accommodates your parent's unique needs. With patience, creativity, and a proactive approach, you can make a significant difference in preserving your parent's cognitive function and overall well-being.

7 FINANCIAL MANAGEMENT: PLANNING FOR THE FUTURE

As a caregiver, managing the financial aspects of your elderly parent's care is crucial for ensuring their well-being and long-term security. This chapter will guide you through the key components of financial management, such as overseeing your parent's assets, understanding insurance options, and creating a budget for their care. By being proactive and informed, you can help safeguard your parent's financial future and alleviate potential stressors related to caregiving.

Managing Your Elderly Parent's Assets

Proper management of your parent's assets can help preserve their financial stability and ensure they have the resources needed to cover the costs of their care. Here are some steps to consider:

- Organize financial records: Gather and organize all essential financial documents, including bank statements, investment accounts, property deeds, insurance policies, and tax records. This will help you gain a clear understanding of your parent's financial situation and make informed decisions.

- Monitor accounts and expenses: Regularly review your parent's bank accounts and track their income and expenses to ensure they are living within their means and avoiding potential financial pitfalls.
- Seek professional advice: Consult with a financial advisor or attorney who specializes in elder law to discuss your parent's financial situation and develop a comprehensive plan for managing their assets.

Understanding Insurance Options

Navigating the various insurance options for elderly parents can be challenging but is essential for securing their health care and financial future. Some insurance options to explore include:

- Medicare: This government-funded health insurance program is available to most individuals aged 65 and older. It covers hospitalization, outpatient care, and prescription medications, with various plans and coverage levels available.
- Medicaid: A state and federal program that provides health insurance for low-income individuals, including elderly parents who meet specific income and asset requirements.
- Long-term care insurance: This type of insurance policy can help cover the costs of long-term care services, such as assisted living, nursing home care, or in-home care.
- Supplemental insurance: Additional insurance policies can help cover expenses not covered by Medicare, such as dental, vision, or hearing care.

Budgeting for Your Elderly Parent's Care

Creating a budget for your parent's care is essential for managing their finances and ensuring they have the resources needed to cover their living and care expenses. To create a budget:

- List all sources of income: Identify all of your parent's income sources, including Social Security, pensions, retirement accounts, and investments.

- Detail monthly expenses: Create a comprehensive list of your parent's monthly expenses, including housing, utilities, food, transportation, medical care, and personal items.

- Compare income and expenses: Assess the difference between your parent's income and their expenses to determine if they are living within their means or if adjustments are needed.

- Identify areas for cost savings: Look for potential cost-saving opportunities, such as consolidating debt, refinancing a mortgage, or downsizing their living situation.

- Plan for future care expenses: Consider the costs of potential long-term care options, such as in-home care, assisted living, or nursing home care, and factor these expenses into your parent's budget.

Financial Assistance and Resources

If your elderly parent requires financial assistance to cover their care expenses, various resources, and programs may be available to help. Some options include:

- Federal and state assistance programs: Investigate programs such as Medicaid, Supplemental Security Income (SSI), or Veterans Affairs (VA) benefits to determine your parent's eligibility for financial assistance.

- Community resources: Local organizations, such as Area Agencies on Aging (AAA) or senior centers, may offer financial assistance, support services, or referral resources for elderly individuals in need of various types of support. These resources may include assistance with housing, utilities, food, transportation, medical care, legal aid, and home modifications or repairs. Additionally, they may provide information on local support groups, recreational activities, and educational programs tailored to the needs of seniors.

Protecting Your Elderly Parent from Financial Abuse

Elder financial abuse is a growing concern, with seniors being particularly vulnerable to scams, fraud, and exploitation. As a caregiver, being vigilant and proactive in protecting your parent's financial well-being is crucial. Some steps to consider include the following:

- Monitor accounts and transactions: Regularly review your parent's financial accounts for any unusual or suspicious activity that could indicate potential fraud or abuse.

- Educate your parent about scams: Inform your elderly parent about common scams targeting seniors, such as telemarketing fraud, phishing emails, and fake charity solicitations. Encourage them to be cautious when sharing personal or financial information.

- Implement safeguards: Set up fraud alerts on your parent's accounts, consider using direct deposit for their income sources, and limit their use of joint accounts to reduce the risk of unauthorized access.

- Consult with professionals: Seek advice from financial advisors, attorneys, or law enforcement agencies if you suspect financial abuse or need guidance on protecting your parent's assets.

Managing the financial aspects of caregiving is a critical responsibility for ensuring your elderly parent's well-being and security. By organizing their financial records, understanding insurance options, creating a budget, exploring available resources, and protecting them from financial abuse, you can help safeguard their financial future and create a stable environment for their care. Remember, seeking professional advice and support can be invaluable in navigating the complex financial landscape of caregiving.

8 LEGAL MATTERS: MAKING SURE ALL THE BASES ARE COVERED

As a caregiver, addressing legal matters is essential to ensure your elderly parent's wishes are respected and their affairs are managed in accordance with their best interests. This chapter will provide an overview of critical legal issues, such as power of attorney, living wills, and guardianship, to help you protect your parent's rights and navigate the legal complexities of caregiving.

Power of Attorney

A power of attorney (POA) is a legal document that grants a designated individual, known as the agent or attorney-in-fact, the authority to make decisions on behalf of your elderly parent, the principal. Establishing a power of attorney can help ensure that your parent's financial, medical, and personal affairs are managed appropriately if they become incapacitated or unable to make decisions independently. There are two main types of power of attorney:

- Financial Power of Attorney: This document authorizes the agent to manage your parent's financial affairs, such as paying bills, filing taxes, and overseeing investments.

- Medical Power of Attorney: Also known as a health care proxy, this document allows the agent to make medical decisions on your parent's behalf if they cannot do so themselves.

Discussing your parent's preferences and involving them in the decision-making process when selecting an agent and drafting a power of attorney is crucial. Consult with an attorney who specializes in elder law to create a power of attorney that meets your parent's specific needs and complies with state laws.

Living Wills and Advance Directives

A living will, also known as an advance directive, is a legal document outlining your elderly parent's preferences regarding medical treatment and end-of-life care if they cannot communicate their wishes. Creating a living will can help alleviate the burden on caregivers and medical professionals by providing clear instructions for managing your parent's health care.

A living will may include information on the following:

- Life-sustaining treatments: Your parent can express their preferences regarding the use of life-sustaining measures, such as resuscitation, ventilation, or artificial nutrition and hydration.

- Palliative care: Your parent can specify their wishes for pain management and comfort care.

- Organ donation: Your parent can indicate their intentions for organ and tissue donation.

- Funeral arrangements: Your parent can outline their preferences for a funeral or memorial services, burial, or cremation.

Consult with an attorney to ensure the living will is legally valid and meets your parent's specific requirements.

Guardianship

Guardianship is a legal process in which a court appoints an individual, known as the guardian, to manage the affairs of an incapacitated or vulnerable person, referred to as the ward. If your elderly parent cannot make decisions independently due to cognitive decline or other health issues, it may be necessary to pursue guardianship. Guardianship can involve:

- Guardianship of the person: The guardian is responsible for making decisions related to the ward's personal care, health, and well-being.
- Guardianship of the estate: The guardian manages the ward's financial affairs and assets.
- Limited guardianship: The court may grant the guardian specific powers or responsibilities, with the ward retaining some decision-making rights.

Guardianship can be complex and time-consuming, requiring court intervention and ongoing oversight. Therefore, it is essential to consider less restrictive alternatives, such as a power of attorney or representative payeeship, before pursuing guardianship. Consult with an attorney experienced in elder law and guardianship to determine the best course of action for your elderly parent.

Elder Law Attorneys

Navigating the legal complexities of caregiving can be challenging, and seeking the assistance of an attorney who specializes in elder law can be invaluable. Elder law attorneys have the expertise to advise you on various caregiving-related issues, such as power of attorney, living wills, guardianship, estate planning, and long-term care planning. They can also help you understand your rights and responsibilities as a caregiver and ensure that your parent's interests are protected.

When selecting an elder law attorney, consider the following:

- Experience: Choose an attorney with a solid background in elder law and a comprehensive understanding of the specific legal issues affecting seniors and their caregivers.
- Reputation: Seek recommendations from friends, family, or professionals in the elder care field.

Research potential attorneys online, read reviews, and check their standing with the local bar association.

- Communication: Look for an attorney who is responsive, patient, and willing to explain complex legal matters clearly and concisely. Ensure they are approachable and open to answering any questions or concerns you may have.
- Fees: Discuss the attorney's fee structure and get an estimate of the total costs involved. Ensure you understand the billing process and any additional expenses that may arise.

Addressing legal matters is a crucial aspect of caregiving, and being well-informed can help ensure your elderly parent's rights and wishes are respected. By establishing a power of attorney, creating a living will, considering guardianship when necessary, and consulting with an elder law attorney, you can confidently navigate the legal challenges of caregiving and provide the best care for your loved one.

9 COPING WITH CHALLENGING BEHAVIORS

Caring for an elderly parent can be emotionally and physically challenging, particularly when they exhibit difficult behaviors due to cognitive decline, mental health issues, or other factors. This chapter aims to guide you on managing these challenging behaviors while maintaining a peaceful and supportive environment for you and your loved one.

Identifying Challenging Behaviors

Challenging behaviors in elderly parents can manifest in various ways, including:

- Aggression: Physical or verbal aggression, including hitting, biting, yelling, or making threats.

- Repetitive behaviors: Repeatedly asking the same questions, pacing, or performing the same tasks over and over.

- Resistance to care: Refusing assistance with personal hygiene, medication, or other essential tasks.

- Wandering: Attempting to leave the home or other care settings without a specific purpose or destination.

- Sleep disturbances: Insomnia, frequent waking, or other sleep disruptions that can lead to fatigue and irritability.
- Mood swings: Rapid shifts in mood or emotional states, such as agitation, anxiety, or depression.

Understanding the possible causes of these behaviors can help you develop appropriate strategies for managing them.

Possible Causes of Challenging Behaviors

Various factors can contribute to challenging behaviors in elderly parents, such as:

- Cognitive decline: Dementia or Alzheimer's disease can cause confusion, memory loss, and difficulty with communication, leading to frustration and challenging behaviors.
- Unmet needs: Your parent may be experiencing physical discomfort, hunger, thirst, or a need for social interaction, which can manifest as challenging behaviors.
- Environmental factors: Overstimulation, unfamiliar surroundings, or lack of routine can lead to increased agitation and challenging behaviors.
- Medication side effects: Some medications can cause mood changes, agitation, or confusion, contributing to challenging behaviors.
- Mental health issues: Depression, anxiety, or other mental health conditions can exacerbate challenging behaviors.

Strategies for Managing Challenging Behaviors

When faced with challenging behaviors, consider the following approaches:

- Remain calm and composed: Keep your voice low and even, maintain a relaxed posture, and avoid sudden movements that may be perceived as threatening.

- Validate their emotions: Acknowledge your parent's feelings and offer reassurance, even if you don't understand the reason for their distress.
- Distract and redirect: Gently shift your parent's focus to a different activity, topic, or environment to help alleviate agitation or frustration.
- Offer choices: Empower your parent by providing options and involving them in decision-making whenever possible.
- Maintain a consistent routine: A predictable daily schedule can help reduce confusion and anxiety for elderly individuals with cognitive decline.
- Modify the environment: Create a safe, comfortable, and calming living space by reducing clutter, noise, and other potential sources of agitation.
- Seek professional support: Consult with your parent's healthcare team to address any underlying medical or mental health issues that may be contributing to challenging behaviors.

Self-Care and Support for Caregivers

Coping with challenging behaviors can be emotionally draining and may lead to caregiver burnout. However, prioritizing self-care and seeking support from friends, family, and professional resources can help you manage your stress and maintain your well-being.

- Set realistic expectations: Accept that you cannot completely control or change your parent's behaviors. Focus on what you can do to support them and create a peaceful environment.
- Practice self-compassion: Recognize that caregiving is a challenging role, and it's normal to feel frustrated, overwhelmed, or upset at times. Be kind to yourself, and remember that you're doing your best under challenging circumstances.

Caregiving is demanding, and it's important to acknowledge your efforts and the love and support you provide to your elderly parent.

Building a Support System

Having a strong support system is essential for managing the challenges of caregiving, including dealing with difficult behaviors. Consider the following strategies for building a network of support:

- Connect with other caregivers: Seek out local caregiver support groups or online forums where you can share experiences, advice, and encouragement with others who understand your challenges.

- Communicate with family and friends: Share your caregiving experiences, concerns, and needs with your loved ones, and be open to their input and assistance.

- Delegate tasks: Be bold and ask for help or delegate caregiving responsibilities to family members, friends, or professional caregivers. Sharing the workload can help reduce your stress and prevent burnout.

- Utilize professional resources: Consult with healthcare professionals, social workers, or geriatric care managers for guidance on managing challenging behaviors and addressing your parent's needs.

- Consider respite care: Arrange for short-term respite care services, such as adult day care or in-home care, to give yourself a break and recharge your energy.

Coping with challenging behaviors in elderly parents can be emotionally taxing and physically demanding. However, by understanding the possible causes, implementing effective strategies, and prioritizing self-care and support, you can manage these behaviors while maintaining a nurturing and peaceful environment for both you and your loved one.

10 THE IMPORTANCE OF SELF-CARE FOR CAREGIVERS

As a caregiver, your primary focus is often on providing the best possible care for your elderly parent. However, neglecting your own well-being can have negative consequences, not only for yourself but also for the person you care for. This chapter emphasizes the importance of self-care for caregivers and offers practical strategies for managing stress, setting boundaries, and finding time for hobbies and relaxation.

The Importance of Self-Care for Caregivers

Self-care is essential for maintaining your physical, emotional, and mental well-being. Failing to prioritize self-care can lead to the following:

- Caregiver burnout: Chronic stress, fatigue, and emotional exhaustion can result in burnout, affecting your ability to provide quality care.

- Health problems: Prolonged stress and lack of self-care can contribute to health issues, such as high blood pressure, heart disease, and a weakened immune system.

- Decreased resilience: Without adequate self-care,

you may become more susceptible to the emotional challenges of caregiving.

- Strained relationships: Neglecting your own needs can lead to feelings of resentment, which may strain your relationships with your elderly parent, family members, and friends.

Managing Stress as a Caregiver

Stress management is a crucial aspect of self-care for caregivers. Consider the following strategies to help reduce stress and promote relaxation:

- Practice mindfulness: Engage in mindfulness exercises, such as deep breathing, progressive muscle relaxation, or meditation, to help calm your mind and reduce stress.

- Exercise regularly: Physical activity can help reduce stress, boost mood, and improve overall well-being. Aim for at least 30 minutes of moderate exercise most days of the week.

- Prioritize sleep: Ensure adequate rest by establishing a consistent sleep schedule and a relaxing bedtime routine.

- Seek support: Share your feelings and experiences with friends, family, or a support group, and be open to receiving help and encouragement.

- Set realistic expectations: Accept that you cannot do everything and that it's okay to ask for help or delegate tasks to others.

Setting Boundaries and Prioritizing Your Needs

Establishing healthy boundaries is essential for maintaining your well-being and preventing burnout. Consider the following tips for setting boundaries and prioritizing your needs:

- Recognize your limits: Be aware of your physical, emotional, and mental limits, and communicate them to others when necessary.

- Learn to say no: Understand that it's okay to

decline additional responsibilities or requests that may compromise your self-care.

- Schedule regular breaks: Set aside time each day for activities that help you recharge and relax, such as reading, taking a walk, or enjoying a hobby.

- Establish a routine: Create a daily routine that includes time for self-care activities and caregiving responsibilities.

- Make time for social connections: Maintain your relationships with friends and family, and prioritize regular social interactions to combat feelings of isolation.

Finding Time for Hobbies and Relaxation

Engaging in hobbies and relaxation activities can help reduce stress and provide a sense of balance in your life. Consider the following suggestions for making time for hobbies and relaxation:

- Schedule leisure time: Just as you schedule caregiving tasks, plan regular intervals for hobbies or relaxation activities.

- Combine socializing with hobbies: Invite friends or family members to join you in your hobbies, which can provide social interaction while also enjoying your interests.

- Explore new interests: Use this opportunity to discover new hobbies or activities that you find enjoyable and fulfilling.

- Prioritize activities that promote relaxation: Choose hobbies or activities that help you unwind and relieve stress. Engaging in activities that bring you joy and promote relaxation can significantly improve your overall well-being and increase your resilience as a caregiver. Some examples of stress-relieving hobbies and activities include:

- Gardening: Tending to plants and nurturing them can provide a sense of accomplishment and a connection to nature, which can be calming.

- Painting or drawing: Creative outlets can help you express your emotions and provide an escape from the demands of caregiving.

- Yoga or Tai Chi: These gentle forms of exercise combine physical movement with mindfulness, promoting relaxation and stress reduction.

- Listening to or playing music: Music can have a soothing effect on the mind and help you process your emotions.

- Reading: Immersing yourself in a good book can provide a mental escape from daily stressors and help you recharge.

- Journaling: Writing about your experiences and emotions can be therapeutic and provide a way to process your thoughts and feelings.

Remember that self-care is not a luxury but a necessity for caregivers. By making time for hobbies, relaxation, and other self-care activities, you can better manage stress and maintain your well-being, enabling you to provide the best possible care for your elderly parent.

In addition to the hobbies and activities mentioned above, here are a few more ideas to help you unwind and relieve stress:

- Cooking or baking: Preparing meals or trying out new recipes can be a creative and therapeutic outlet that also provides nourishment for you and your loved one.

- Walking or hiking: Enjoying a leisurely walk or hike in nature can help clear your mind, reduce stress, and improve your physical health.

- Crafting: Engaging in various crafts, such as knitting, sewing, or woodworking, can provide a sense of accomplishment and a creative outlet.

- Meditation: Practicing meditation can help you cultivate mindfulness, reduce stress, and improve your emotional well-being.

- Volunteering: Giving back to your community can provide a sense of purpose and connection while helping you take a break from your caregiving responsibilities.
- Joining a club or group: Participating in a group that shares your interests, such as a book club, photography group, or sports team, can provide social interaction and an opportunity to pursue your passions.
- Taking classes or attending workshops: Learning something new or developing a skill can be both stimulating and rewarding while also providing a break from caregiving duties.
- Traveling: Taking short trips or vacations can offer a much-needed change of scenery and an opportunity to recharge.
- Watching movies or attending theater performances: Engaging in cultural activities can provide entertainment and relaxation.
- Practicing gratitude: Focusing on the positive aspects of your life and expressing gratitude can help shift your mindset and reduce stress.

By exploring various hobbies and activities, you can find what best suits your interests and needs for relaxation and stress relief. Maintaining a balance between caregiving responsibilities and self-care will help ensure that you remain healthy, resilient, and able to provide the best possible care for your elderly parent.

11 BUILDING A SUPPORT SYSTEM: FRIENDS, FAMILY, AND PROFESSIONALS

As a caregiver, having a strong support system is essential for maintaining your well-being and ensuring that you can provide the best care possible for your elderly parent. While caregiving can be a rewarding experience, it can also be emotionally, physically, and mentally draining. By establishing a reliable network of friends, family, and professionals, you can alleviate some of the burdens associated with caregiving, share your experiences, and gain access to valuable resources.

The Importance of a Support System

- Emotional support: Caregiving can be an emotionally challenging journey. A support system provides a safe space to share your feelings, experiences, and concerns with others who can empathize and offer encouragement.
- Practical assistance: Friends, family, and professional caregivers can offer help with daily tasks, such as running errands, preparing meals, or providing respite care to give you a much-needed break.
- Information and resources: A support system can provide access to valuable information, advice, and resources related to caregiving, including legal, financial, and healthcare matters.
- Validation and reassurance: Connecting with

others who share similar experiences can help validate your feelings and provide reassurance that you are not alone in your caregiving journey.

Enlisting Friends and Family

- Communicate your needs: Be open and honest with your friends and family about the challenges you face as a caregiver and the type of support you require. Don't be afraid to ask for help when needed.

- Share responsibilities: Divide caregiving tasks among friends and family members based on their strengths, availability, and interests. This can help alleviate the burden and create a team approach to caregiving.

- Establish a support group: Create a group of friends and family members who can regularly meet or communicate to discuss caregiving challenges and share advice, information, and emotional support.

- Encourage involvement: Invite friends and family to spend time with your elderly parent and participate in activities to foster a sense of community and inclusiveness.

Connecting with Professional Caregivers

- Respite care: Professional caregivers can provide temporary relief by stepping in to care for your elderly parent, allowing you to rest and recharge.

- Home care services: Skilled professionals can assist with various caregiving tasks, such as personal care, meal preparation, medication management, and companionship.

- Adult daycare centers: These facilities offer structured programs and activities for seniors, providing socialization and stimulation while giving caregivers a break.

- Geriatric care managers: These professionals can assess your parent's needs, coordinate care services, and provide guidance on various aspects of caregiving.

Joining Support Groups and Online Communities

- Local support groups: Many communities have caregiver support groups that meet regularly, providing an opportunity to connect with others who share similar experiences and challenges.

- Online support communities: There are numerous online forums, social media groups, and websites dedicated to caregiving where you can ask questions, share advice, and find emotional support.

- Disease-specific groups: If your parent has a specific condition, such as Alzheimer's, Parkinson's, or cancer, there may be support groups tailored to the unique challenges associated with that disease.

- Educational workshops and seminars: Attending workshops or seminars related to caregiving can help you gain valuable knowledge and connect with other caregivers.

Utilizing Community Resources

- Area Agencies on Aging (AAA): These organizations provide a range of support services for seniors and caregivers, such as information and referral services, legal assistance, and transportation.

- Senior centers: Local senior centers offer various activities, resources, and programs designed to promote socialization and engagement for elderly individuals. These centers can provide your elderly parent with opportunities to make new friends, participate in recreational activities, and access valuable resources while giving you some respite from caregiving duties.

- Non-profit organizations: Numerous non-profit organizations are dedicated to providing support and resources for caregivers and seniors. These organizations may offer information, financial assistance, respite care, and other services that can help lighten your caregiving load.

- Faith-based communities: Many religious organizations offer support for caregivers and seniors, including support groups, respite care, and social activities. Connecting with your faith-based community can provide spiritual and emotional support for both you and your elderly parent.

Building a strong support system is crucial for managing the challenges associated with caregiving. By involving friends, family, professionals, and community resources, you can create a network of support that not only benefits your elderly parent but also helps you maintain your well-being and emotional health. Remember, caregiving is a team effort; you don't have to do it alone. Reach out to those around you, and you'll find that the journey becomes more manageable and fulfilling for everyone involved.

- Online support groups and forums: The internet provides numerous opportunities for caregivers to connect with others who are going through similar experiences. Online support groups and forums can be valuable information, advice, and emotional support sources. These platforms allow you to share your experiences, ask questions, and gain insights from other caregivers who have faced similar challenges.

- Professional counseling: Seeking the guidance of a professional counselor or therapist can be beneficial for caregivers who are struggling with the emotional and mental aspects of their role. A professional can provide coping strategies, guidance, and support to help you navigate the complex emotions associated with caregiving.

- Educational resources and workshops: Many organizations offer workshops, seminars, and courses designed to educate and support caregivers. These educational opportunities can provide you with practical knowledge and skills to help you better manage your caregiving responsibilities.

- Respite care services: Respite care is a service that allows caregivers to take a temporary break from their duties while ensuring that their elderly parent is well cared for. Many organizations and agencies offer respite care services, either in-home or at specialized facilities. Utilizing respite care can help you maintain your well-being and avoid caregiver burnout.

By exploring and utilizing these various support resources, you can build a robust support system that will help you navigate the challenging journey of caregiving. Remember, you don't have to face this journey alone. By reaching out and seeking support from friends, family, professionals, and community resources, you can create a more balanced and fulfilling caregiving experience for both you and your elderly parent.

12 THE CAREGIVER'S GUIDE TO PREPARING FOR THE END - GRIEF, LOSS, AND ACCEPTANCE

As a caregiver, it can be challenging to confront the reality that your elderly loved one's journey is coming to an end. Preparing for the end-of-life stage is an emotionally and mentally exhausting experience, but it's a necessary part of the caregiving journey. This chapter provides guidance on coping with grief, loss, and acceptance, as well as practical advice on preparing for the end-of-life stage.

Understanding the End-of-Life Stage

The end-of-life stage is a natural part of the aging process. As your elderly loved one approaches the end of their life, they may experience physical and cognitive decline, increased frailty, and a reduced quality of life. The end-of-life stage can be emotionally challenging for both the elderly individual and their caregivers, as it often involves coping with loss and preparing for the inevitable.

Coping with Grief and Loss

Grief and loss are natural emotions that caregivers and their elderly loved ones may experience during the end-of-life stage. As a caregiver, it's essential to acknowledge and validate these emotions for yourself and your loved one. Some common emotions associated with grief and loss include sadness, anger, guilt, and fear.

To cope with these emotions, it's important to:

- Acknowledge your emotions: Allow yourself to feel them and express them healthily. Consider journaling, talking to a trusted friend or family member, or seeking the guidance of a professional counselor.
- Practice self-care: Take care of your physical, emotional, and mental well-being. Sleep well, eat a healthy diet, and engage in activities that bring joy and relaxation.
- Seek support: Reach out to friends, family, and other caregivers for emotional support. Consider joining a support group or seeking professional counseling.

Preparing for the End-of-Life Stage

Preparing for the end-of-life stage can be an emotionally difficult process, but it's an important part of ensuring that your elderly loved one's wishes are respected and that they receive the best possible care. Some practical steps you can take to prepare for the end-of-life stage include:

- Have conversations about end-of-life care: Discuss your elderly loved one's wishes for end-of-life care, such as whether they prefer to be at home or in a hospice facility and what kind of medical interventions they do or do not want.

- Review legal documents: Ensure that your elderly loved one's legal documents, such as their will, power of attorney, and living will, are up-to-date and reflect their current wishes.

- Plan for funeral arrangements: Consider pre-planning funeral arrangements with your elderly loved one to ensure their wishes are respected and reduce the burden on caregivers during an already emotionally challenging time.

- Consider hospice care: Hospice care is a specialized type of care designed to provide comfort and support to individuals in the end-of-life stage. Consider whether hospice care is an appropriate option for your elderly loved one.

Accepting the End-of-Life Stage

Accepting the end-of-life stage can be challenging, but it's an important part of finding peace and closure. Acceptance involves acknowledging that death is a natural part of the life cycle and that your loved one's journey is coming to an end. Some ways to find acceptance include:

- Engage in spiritual or religious practices: Many caregivers and their elderly loved ones find comfort in spiritual or religious practices, such as prayer or meditation.

- Focus on the present moment: Rather than dwelling on the past or worrying about the future, focus on enjoying the present moment with your loved one.

- Practice gratitude: Focus on the positive memories and experiences.

- Seek support: Surround yourself with loved ones, friends, and caregivers who can provide emotional support during this difficult time.

Find meaning and purpose: Consider finding

meaning and purpose in your loved one's journey by engaging in activities or causes that align with their values or passions.

Caring for an elderly loved one during the end-of-life stage can be emotionally and mentally challenging, but it's an important part of the caregiving journey. By preparing for the end-of-life stage, coping with grief and loss, and finding acceptance, caregivers can provide the best possible care for their loved ones while taking care of their emotional and mental well-being. Remember to seek support, practice self-care, and take things one day at a time.

- Make necessary arrangements: In addition to emotional preparation, it's important to make practical arrangements such as advance directives, funeral arrangements, and legal matters.

- Seek professional support: Consider seeking hospice care or other healthcare professionals specializing in end-of-life care. They can provide guidance, support, and resources for both the caregiver and the elderly loved one.

- Practice self-care: Caregivers must prioritize their emotional and mental well-being during this challenging time. This includes engaging in self-care activities such as exercise, meditation, and spending time with loved ones.

- Address unfinished business: Encourage your loved one to address any unfinished business, such as making amends or expressing gratitude to loved ones.

- Reflect and remember: After your loved one passes, take time to reflect and remember the memories and moments shared. This can include creating a memory box, scrapbook, or other meaningful keepsakes.

It's important to remember that grief is a unique and

personal experience, and everyone copes with it in their own way. It's okay to seek professional support, talk to loved ones, and take time for yourself during this challenging time. Remember to be patient and kind with yourself and allow yourself to grieve in your own way.

Stay organized: Keeping track of important documents, medical records, and financial information can be overwhelming during the end-of-life stage. Consider creating a system or using a binder or file to keep everything organized and easily accessible.

- Address spiritual needs: For some elderly individuals and their families, addressing spiritual needs during the end-of-life stage can be significant. This may include religious or spiritual practices, such as prayer, meditation, or visits from spiritual leaders.

- Address cultural needs: Different cultures have unique customs and beliefs surrounding death and dying. It's essential to understand and respect these cultural practices and consider how they may impact caregiving and the end-of-life process.

- Take breaks: Caring for an elderly loved one during the end-of-life stage can be emotionally and physically exhausting. Caregivers must take breaks, whether through respite care or enlisting the help of family and friends.

- Seek closure: After your loved one passes, it can be helpful to seek closure through rituals or traditions that have personal significance. This may include holding a memorial service, scattering ashes in a meaningful location, or creating a special tribute.

Caregivers need to approach the end-of-life stage with compassion, empathy, and an open mind. By being prepared, seeking support, and prioritizing self-care, caregivers can provide their elderly loved ones with the best possible care while taking care of themselves.

- Communicate openly: Communication is key during the end-of-life stage, both with the elderly loved one and with other family members and caregivers. Be honest and open about what to expect and address any concerns or questions.

- Consider alternative therapies: Alternative therapies, such as music or art therapy, can be helpful in providing comfort and promoting emotional well-being for both the elderly loved one and the caregiver.

- Make the most of the time remaining: While it can be challenging to stay present during the end-of-life stage, it's important to make the most of the time remaining with your loved one. This may include spending quality time together, creating meaningful memories, or addressing unresolved issues.

- Accept help: Accepting help from others, whether it's from family members, friends, or professionals, can help alleviate some of the burdens of caregiving and provide much-needed support during this difficult time.

- Celebrate life: Although the end-of-life stage can be filled with sadness and grief, it's important to celebrate the life and legacy of your loved one. This can include sharing stories, looking through old photos, or hosting a celebration of life event after their passing.

- Address end-of-life preferences: It's important to have conversations with your elderly loved one about their end-of-life preferences, including whether they would like to receive life-prolonging treatments, where they would like to spend their final days, and their wishes regarding funeral arrangements.

- Seek professional support: Seeking support from professionals, such as hospice care providers, can help ensure that your loved one's end-of-life needs are met and can also provide emotional support for the caregiver and family members.

- Address legal matters: It's vital to ensure that all legal matters, such as wills, trusts, and advance directives, are in order and up-to-date during the end-of-life stage.

- Be prepared for the grieving process: Grieving is a natural and normal process after the death of a loved one. However, it's important to be prepared for the grieving process and to seek support from family members, friends, or professionals as needed.

- Remember self-care: Self-care is vital during the end-of-life stage for both the elderly loved one and the caregiver. This may include finding time for relaxation and self-care activities, seeking support from others, and taking care of one's physical and emotional well-being.

- Practice self-compassion: Caregiving during the end-of-life stage can be emotionally and physically taxing. It's important to practice self-compassion, which involves being kind and understanding towards yourself and recognizing that caregiving is a challenging role.

- Seek spiritual support: For some individuals and families, spiritual support can be an important aspect of the end-of-life stage. This may involve seeking guidance and comfort from religious leaders, participating in spiritual practices, or finding comfort in spiritual beliefs.

- Prepare for the future: After the passing of a loved one, there may be various practical matters that need to be addressed, such as managing the estate and notifying relevant parties. It's important to prepare for these tasks in advance and seek support from professionals or family members as needed.

Continue to seek support: The end-of-life stage can be a difficult and emotional time, and the grieving process may continue for some time after the passing of a loved one. It's important to continue seeking support from others, whether it's from friends, family, support groups, or professionals.

Remember to honor your loved one's memory: After the passing of a loved one, it's important to find ways to honor and remember their life and legacy. This may include creating a memorial, participating in rituals or traditions that were important to them, or finding other meaningful ways to honor their memory.

13 THE ENDURING ROLE OF CAREGIVING: SUPPORTING YOUR ELDERLY PARENT THROUGH LIFE'S TRANSITIONS

Caring for an elderly loved one is a significant responsibility that can involve a range of emotional, physical, financial, and legal challenges. Throughout this guide, we have explored the various types of care and support that may be necessary during the caregiving journey, as well as tips and strategies for managing the common challenges that may arise.

In Chapter 1, we discussed the importance of understanding the different types of care, including in-home care, assisted living, and nursing home care. Each option has its own benefits and drawbacks, and it's important to consider factors such as your loved one's health status, budget, and personal preferences when deciding which type of care is most appropriate.

Chapter 2 emphasized the importance of accepting your role as a caregiver and coping with the various emotions and challenges that may arise. This includes managing stress, seeking support from others, and practicing self-care to ensure that you are able to provide the best care possible for your loved one.

Chapter 3 delved into the physical needs of elderly parents, including maintaining their personal hygiene, managing medications, and preparing nutritious meals. By ensuring that your loved one's physical needs are met, you can help promote their overall health and well-being.

Chapter 4 explored the importance of emotional care, including building a strong emotional bond with your loved one through empathy, patience, and communication. Providing emotional support and companionship can be just as important as meeting your loved one's physical needs.

Chapter 5 highlighted the importance of cognitive care, including providing mentally stimulating activities and resources to help keep your loved one's mind sharp and engaged.

Chapter 6 discussed the financial aspects of caregiving, including managing your loved one's assets, understanding insurance options, and budgeting for their care.

Chapter 7 explored the essential legal matters for caregivers, such as creating a power of attorney and establishing a living will.

In Chapter 8, we discussed strategies for managing challenging behaviors that may arise due to cognitive decline or other factors.

Chapter 9 emphasized the importance of self-care for caregivers, including managing stress, setting boundaries, and finding time for hobbies and relaxation.

Chapter 10 discussed the importance of building a

support system, including seeking support from friends, family, and professionals.

Chapter 11 provided guidance on preparing for the end-of-life stage, including addressing end-of-life preferences, seeking professional support, and addressing legal matters.

Finally, in Chapter 12, we discussed the grieving process and strategies for coping with grief and loss after the passing of a loved one.

As you navigate the caregiving journey, it's important to remember that no two experiences are the same. Each family and caregiving situation is unique, and it's important to be flexible and adaptable as you navigate the various challenges that may arise. By providing the best care possible for your loved one and practicing self-care and self-compassion, you can help ensure that you and your loved one can navigate this journey with grace and dignity. In addition to the topics covered in each chapter, it's important to recognize that the caregiving journey can be unpredictable and may require flexibility and adaptability. For example, your loved one's health status may change unexpectedly, or you may need to adjust your care plan based on their evolving needs.

It's also important to recognize that caregiving can be a long-term commitment, and it's important to plan for the future. This may include thinking about long-term care options, such as assisted living or nursing home care, or discussing end-of-life preferences with your loved one.

Furthermore, caregiving can be emotionally challenging, and it's important to recognize that asking for help is okay. Seeking support from friends, family, and professionals can help ease the burden of caregiving and provide much-needed emotional support.

Finally, it's important to recognize that caregiving is a role that is often taken on out of love and compassion for a loved one. While it can be a difficult and challenging journey, it can also be a rewarding and fulfilling experience that allows you to deepen your relationship with your loved one and create meaningful memories together. In addition to the points mentioned above, it's important to recognize that every caregiving situation is unique and may require different approaches and strategies. What works for one caregiver or elderly parent may not necessarily work for another.

Therefore, it's important to approach caregiving with an open mind and a willingness to learn and adapt. This may require seeking additional resources and support, such as attending support groups or consulting healthcare professionals.

It's also essential to prioritize your own health and well-being as a caregiver. This means taking the time to care for yourself physically and emotionally and seeking help or support when needed. Neglecting your own needs can lead to burnout and make it more difficult to provide adequate care for your loved one.

Finally, it's crucial to maintain open and honest communication with your loved one throughout the caregiving journey. This may involve discussing their preferences, fears, and concerns and sharing your thoughts and feelings. By fostering a strong and open relationship, you can work together to navigate the challenges of caregiving and ensure the best possible care for your elderly parent. Another vital aspect to consider when providing care for an elderly parent is the impact on other relationships and responsibilities in your life. Caregiving can be time-consuming and emotionally demanding, and it's important to ensure that you are still able to fulfill other roles and responsibilities, such as being a parent or a spouse or maintaining a career.

This may require setting boundaries and seeking out additional help or support, such as hiring a caregiver or enlisting the help of other family members. It's important to recognize that you don't have to do everything alone and that asking for help or taking a break is okay when needed.

Additionally, addressing any legal or financial concerns early on in the caregiving journey is important. This may involve creating a will, establishing a power of attorney, or setting up a trust to manage your parent's assets. By addressing these concerns early on, you can help prevent legal or financial issues from arising down the line.

Finally, it's important to recognize that caregiving is a valuable and important role that is often taken on out of love and compassion for a loved one. By providing care for an elderly parent, you are helping them to maintain their independence and dignity while also creating meaningful memories and deepening your relationship with them. Another important aspect to consider is the potential impact of caregiving on your own mental health. Caregiving can be a stressful and emotional experience, and it's important to recognize when you may need additional support or resources to cope.

This may involve seeking counseling or therapy to address feelings of anxiety, depression, or burnout or joining a support group to connect with other caregivers who are going through similar experiences. It's important to prioritize your mental health and well-being to provide adequate care for your loved one.

Another consideration is the potential impact of caregiving on your own physical health. Caregiving can be physically demanding, and it's crucial to ensure that you are taking care of your own health by getting enough sleep, eating a healthy diet, and engaging in regular physical activity.

It's also important to recognize that caregiving can be a long-term commitment and that the needs of your elderly parent may change over time. As such, it's important to remain flexible and open to adjusting your care plan to ensure your loved one receives the best possible care.

In conclusion, caregiving for an elderly parent can be a challenging and rewarding experience. However, by understanding their needs, building a strong support system, and prioritizing your own health and well-being, you can provide adequate care and create meaningful memories with your loved one. One more critical aspect to consider is the importance of communication in caregiving. Clear and open communication with your elderly parent can help establish trust, build a strong relationship, and ensure that their needs and preferences are being met.

It's also important to communicate effectively with other family members, healthcare professionals, and other caregivers involved in your loved one's care. This may involve regular check-ins to discuss changes in your parent's health or needs and sharing information about medications, appointments, and other important details.

By prioritizing effective communication and working together as a team, you can help ensure your loved one receives the best possible care and support.

ABOUT THE AUTHOR

Jill Wyatt is a certified nursing assistant with experience in long-term care and mental health care. She is currently pursuing her nursing degree at Galen College of Nursing. These experiences, along with witnessing her mother's struggles when they decided to move her grandmother into their home, inspired Jill to share her knowledge and insights with others through her writing, including her book Tender Hearts: Navigating the Journey of Caring for an Elderly Parent or Grandparent. Jill's passion for providing compassionate care and support to the elderly and their caregivers is evident in her writing. When she's not studying, writing, or caring for her family and loved ones, Jill enjoys spending time with her five dogs and engaging in outdoor activities.